WILD ANIMAL BABIES

RABBIT KITS

NOAH RICCARDI

PowerKiDS press

Published in 2027 by The Rosen Publishing Group, Inc.
2544 Clinton Street, Buffalo, NY 14224

First Edition

Book Design: Marley Richmond

Photo Credits: Cover, p. 1 Red Grouse/Shutterstock.com; p. 5 Yousuf Dean/Shutterstock.com; p. 7 Braga Pictures/Shutterstock.com; p. 9 Peyker/Shutterstock.com; p. 11 Lindasj22/Shutterstock.com; p. 13 Taris Atamaniv/Shutterstock.com; p. 15 Suriya Chan/Shutterstock.com; p. 17 Capo Hiena/Shutterstock.com; p. 19 Leena Robinson/Shutterstock.com; p. 21 Helen J. Davies/Shutterstock.com.

Cataloging-in-Publication Data
Names: Riccardi, Noah.
Title: Rabbit kits / Noah Riccardi.
Description: Buffalo, New York : PowerKids Press, 2027. | Series: Wild animal babies | Includes glossary and index.
Identifiers: ISBN 9781538295519 (pbk.) | ISBN 9781538295526 (library bound) | ISBN 9781538295533 (ebook)
Subjects: LCSH: Rabbits--Infancy--Juvenile literature.
Classification: LCC QL737.L32 R533 2027 | DDC 599.321392--dc23

Manufactured in China

CPSIA Compliance Information: Batch #QS27PK. For Further Information contact Rosen Publishing, at 1-800-237-9932.

CONTENTS

All About Rabbits 4

Early Days 6

Nest Life 10

Wandering Out 14

Growing Up Fast 18

Circle of Life 20

Glossary 22

For More Information 23

Index 24

All About Rabbits

Rabbits are small **mammals** known for their long ears. They live all over the world. Rabbits are **herbivores**. They live by eating grasses and other plants. The name for a baby rabbit is a kit.

Early Days

Rabbits are born in **litters** of up to 14 kits. They are born completely helpless. The newborn kits are blind, deaf, and **bald**. They weigh 1 to 3.5 ounces (28 to 99 g).

Kits start to grow fur around their third day. By one week, they have a full layer of thin fur. Kits also grow very quickly. They double their weight in their first week.

Nest Life

The mother rabbit, or **doe**, digs a nest for her kits. This nest is a small **ditch** dug into grassy ground. The doe leaves her kits in the nest. She tops it with some fur or grass.

Newborn kits hide in the nest. They depend on their mother for food. The doe visits once or twice each day to **nurse** her kits. She leaves them alone the rest of the day.

Wandering Out

By two weeks, the kits fully open their eyes. They now have a coat of fur. They still live in the nest for a few more weeks. Their mother still feeds them.

When they are around two to three weeks old, kits leave the nest for the first time. They go out to eat some grass. Then they come back to the nest. They stay there for a little longer.

Growing Up Fast

After four weeks, kits are **weaned**. They can feed themselves enough to survive. Kits start to leave the nest at this age. They are still small. But they can live on their own.

Circle of Life

A doe can have many litters in one year. Once her kits leave the nest, she can have another litter. Her young rabbits keep growing, too. When they are four to five months old, they can have their own kits.

GLOSSARY

bald: Without any fur or hair.

ditch: A hole in the ground.

doe: An adult female rabbit.

herbivores: Animals that eat only plants.

litters: Groups of baby rabbits born at the same time.

mammals: Animals that have hair or fur and that feed milk to their babies.

nurse: When a mother feeds kits milk from her body.

weaned: Not needing to nurse for food anymore.

FOR MORE INFORMATION

BOOKS

An, Priscilla. *Rabbit Behavior*. Minneapolis, MN: Abdo Publishing, 2024.

Howell, Izzi. *Rabbits*. Buffalo, NY: Rosen Publishing, 2025.

WEBSITES

Britannica Kids: Rabbit and Hare
kids.britannica.com/kids/article/rabbit-and-hare/353689
Learn more about rabbits and hares at this website.

National Geographic Kids: Eastern Cottontail Rabbit
kids.nationalgeographic.com/animals/mammals/facts/eastern-cottontail-rabbit
Learn more about the eastern cottontail, a very common species of rabbit.

INDEX

B
baldness, 6
blindness, 6

D
deafness, 6
ditches, 10
does, 10, 12, 20

F
feeding, 14, 18
fur, 8, 10, 14

G
grasses, 4, 10, 16
growth, 8, 20

L
litters, 6, 20

M
mammals, 4

N
nests, 10, 12, 14, 16, 18, 20
newborns, 6, 12
nursing, 12

S
survival, 18

W
weaning, 18